Who Am I?

30 Daily Encounters with God

"Where questioning ends…and your real identity begins."

"Realize who you are, whose you are, and position yourself to walk in your purpose"

God has created everyone for a purpose. People spend their whole lives wondering why they are here; many dying without operating in their God-given destiny. In order to know your purpose, you must first know who you are. In order to know your true identity, you must consult with the one who created you, God. On this 30-day journey of quiet encounter with your Heavenly Father, you will realize your true identity, authority, and be able to position yourself for God to reveal to you the reason he has placed you on this earth.

Dedicated to.... You

If I only inspire one, encourage one, or empower one person to know that you are a valuable, rare treasure carefully crafted by your Heavenly Father, positioned as royalty, I have multiplied God's kingdom on the earth.

Love,
Takenya

Contents

Contents iv
You are Loved! 1
You are Valuable! 7
You're Uniquely and Wonderfully Made! 15
You are Gifted and Destined for Greatness! 23
You are Powerful! 31
You are a King or Queen! 39
You are God's Strong Mighty Warrior! 47
You are Victorious! 55
You are a Lady or Gentleman! 63
You are a Blessing to Others! 71
You are Royalty! 79
You are Loved! 87
You are Valuable! 95
You are Uniquely and Wonderfully Made! 103
You are Gifted! 111
You are Destined for Greatness! 119
You are Powerful! 127
You are a King or Queen! 135
You are God's Strong Mighty Warrior! 143
You are Victorious! 151
You are a Lady or Gentleman! 159
You are a Blessing to Others! 167
You are Royalty! 175
You are Loved! 183
You are Valuable! 191

You are Uniquely and Wonderfully Made! 199
You are Gifted and Destined for Greatness! 207
You are a Powerful King or Queen! 215
You are God's Strong Mighty Warrior! You are Victorious! .. 223
You are a Lady or Gentleman, a Blessing to Others! You are Royalty! 231

WHO AM I DAILY ENCOUNTERS

My child, I know what you are going through. I want you to know that regardless of your situation I love you! Spend 10 minutes with me each day to discover just how much!

Love, Your Heavenly Father

Day 1

You are Loved!

For God so loved the world that he gave his one and only Son, that whoever believes in him shall not perish but have eternal life.

John 3:16

FROM YOUR FATHER

Darling I love you so much! I love you more than you love Chipotle or social media. I allowed my ONLY Son to be sacrificed and die for YOU! My hope is that you realize the depth of my love for you. I don't want you to choose things that will get you in trouble, but as your loving daddy, my desire is for you to choose to believe in Jesus and my love for you.

Day 1

THINK ABOUT

What do you spend most of your time thinking about or doing? Why? Probably because you really enjoy it. Can you imagine God scrolling on Instagram or YouTube all day looking at pictures of you and watching videos of you? He does! He thinks about you all day and night!

How does knowing that God is thinking about you all of the time make you feel?

TAKE AWAY

Know that God loves you more than you could ever love anything or anyone else! You are always on His mind!!

"YOU ARE LOVED."

Day 1

MONTH 1

Day 1

Day 1

MONTH 2

Day 1

Day 1

MONTH 3

Day 1

Day 2

You are Valuable!

"See what an incredible quality of love the Father has shown to us, that we would [be permitted to] be named and called and counted the children of God! And so we are! For this reason the world does not know us, because it did not know Him."

1 JOHN 3:1 AMP

FROM YOUR FATHER

My child, true love is an action. Not only did I show my love by sacrificing my Son for you, but my love covers you as I am your father. You are my child. You have my last name and my blood running through your veins. This means that you are a reflection of Me. I have chosen you and brought you into my family; not treating as a stepchild, but as the one I birthed; My very own!

Day 2

THINK ABOUT

When Adam sinned, we were separated from a relationship with God. Imagine your father leaving you. You feel rejected, lonely, and not being able to sit on his lap when you're scared, or talk to him when you need guidance. You feel unwanted and invaluable. That is not love. God is the opposite type of daddy. He handpicked you to be his child, even knowing your flaws and bad choices. He chose you to be an heir to his kingdom! You are royalty!

What is it that others have spoken over you that goes against what God is telling you? Knowing now that your last name is Royalty, what can you do to live up to your position?

TAKE AWAY

Even knowing all of your flaws and bad choices, God still chose you to be His child. He didn't just allow you to be a part of His family because He had to, He chose you because He wanted to! You have His last name, Royalty! What can you do to live up to your position?

"YOU ARE VALUABLE."

Day 2
MONTH 1

Day 2

Day 2
MONTH 2

Day 2

Day 2

MONTH 3

Day 2

Day 3

You're Uniquely and Wonderfully Made!

> 5 "Before I formed you, before you were born, I set you apart; in the womb I knew and appointed you as a prophet to the nations."
>
> Jeremiah 1:5

FROM YOUR FATHER

You are not an accident. I thought of you long before your mother birthed you. I purposefully created you exactly how I wanted. I gave you purpose and destiny like no one else. After imagining you in my mind, I am the one who formed you with my hands while you were in your mother's stomach. My child, I KNOW YOU...your thoughts, desires, choices you'll make, and even your fears and I still love you!

Day 3

THINK ABOUT

Your mother has a connection to you that no one else has. She loves you with an unconditional love. Nothing can take that love away. Even more than her love for you, is God's love for you. His connection to you is even stronger. He knows you inside and out. He values you so much that he carefully formed you, not just threw you together at the last minute. He hand-picked your character traits and what he wants you to do in life. That takes a lot of thought and careful planning. You are so valuable and special to God, your daddy! He also chose your mom to be your mom. That was no accident!

God is a God of growth and transformation. Write down your new mindset you are programming into your heart and brain. Describe something you previously thought was bad about you, that God says is wonderful.

TAKE AWAY

You are not an afterthought. You were on God's mind way before the earth existed. He planned, prepared, and handcrafted you. He knows you and chose you to be someone great! He's your father.

"YOU ARE UNIQUELY AND WONDERFULLY MADE."

Day 3

MONTH 1

Day 3

Day 3

MONTH 2

Day 3

Day 3

MONTH 3

Day 3

Day 4

You are Gifted and Destined for Greatness!

I, the LORD, have called you for a righteous purpose, and I will take hold of your hand. I will keep you and appoint you to be a covenant for the people and a light to the nations...

Isaiah 42:6

FROM YOUR FATHER

My child, I created you for a great purpose with a unique gift only you have. Your life matters. I am sending you out to impact the lives of many by stirring up the gift inside of you. You have been born into the right family, at the right time, to utilize the natural talent I've placed inside of you. People are waiting for you to walk in your destiny. You are their promise for a better life. You are to bring hope to their hopeless situation.

Day 4

THINK ABOUT

You were created for more. You're not an Ordinary person, but the almighty God, your daddy, created you to impact people's lives for good. Use your position of power and authority as the King's child to be a positive influence to those around you. People look up to you.

Journal characteristics about your family, parents and life you don't like. Write down what is going on in our society right now that isn't so great. What are you good at naturally?

TAKE AWAY

You are called for a great purpose; to impact many people for good.

"YOU ARE GIFTED AND DESTINED FOR GREATNESS."

Day 4

MONTH 1

Day 4

Day 4

MONTH 2

Day 4

Day 4

MONTH 3

Day 4

Day 5

You are Powerful!

"So God created human beings in his own image. In the image of God he created them; male and female he created them. Then God blessed them and said, "Be fruitful and multiply. Fill the earth and govern it. Reign over the fish in the sea, the birds in the sky, and all the animals that scurry along the ground."

Genesis 1:27-28 NLT

FROM YOUR FATHER

Like Father like daughter. I made you just like me. My blood and genes are running through you. Like me, I want you to be loving, kind, helpful, and patient. Show others my good character and people will want what you have: me inside of you. You are strong and powerful. I made you to be a ruler. Inside of you is leadership potential. You have a strong will, but make sure your desires line up with mine.

Day 5

THINK ABOUT

"You get it from your daddy…" God designed you to be like Himself: sensitive, yet strong-willed, a person that enjoys helping others, but also a leader. You are powerful; called to rule/lead in your circle of influence. You are the child of the King!

What will you do with your authority? Will you use it for good or evil? Write down one way you can be the same kind of leader, in your circle of influence like your daddy. What area do people tend to follow you, or look to you? How can you use your power of influence for God?

TAKE AWAY

People are watching and following you.

"YOU ARE POWERFUL"

Day 5

MONTH 1

Day 5

Day 5

MONTH 2

Day 5

Day 5
MONTH 3

Day 5

Day 6

You are a King or Queen!

"But you are not like that, for you are a chosen people. You are royal priests, a holy nation, God's very own possession. As a result, you can show others the goodness of God, for he called you out of the darkness into his wonderful light."

1 Peter 2:9NLT

FROM YOUR FATHER

I've chosen you. I've appointed you to become King. You are to be different than your friends and the society you live in. As royalty, you are required to behave and talk a certain way: proper with my morals and values. The world is looking up to you. They follow what you do. Show my goodness to those around you. You are my very own special treasure!

Day 6

THINK ABOUT

When you watch Princess Diaries or the Royal family, how do they present themselves? Are they allowed to talk any kind of way? Dress any kind of way? People of royal descent are raised to have good manners and etiquette. They influence so many people and can lead them down the wrong path. As royalty, your choices, attitude, and appearance represent your family name. It is the same with you. Because you are the child of the King, you're required to represent God's kingdom to the best. You are to talk, act, and have the same heart He does because you influence the lives of so many people.

What are three things you can change in regards to your speech, behavior or appearance to look more like your Father, The King?!

TAKE AWAY

You are royalty. Act like.

"YOU ARE A KING/QUEEN!"

Day 6

MONTH 1

Day 6

Day 6

MONTH 2

Day 6

Day 6

MONTH 3

Day 6

Day 7

You are God's Strong Mighty Warrior!

The LORD said to Joshua, "Do not be afraid of them; I have given them into your hand. Not one of them will be able to withstand you.
Joshua 10:8

FROM YOUR FATHER

You have an enemy that's after your life and all of the blessings I have in store for you! He wants you to believe that what he offers is better than my love. Don't believe his lies. He offers a counterfeit love that doesn't last. The friends, popularity, acceptance, and attention that comes with his offer is contingent upon your allegiance to him. Don't follow your friends or what the world says is good; it will only lead you to destruction. Don't be afraid of losing friends for following me. You are my child. You have authority. You are a part of my army. With me you have victory. You are my strong mighty warrior!

Day 7

THINK ABOUT

The battles you face with your friends, peer pressure, the need to feel accepted and important, come from the enemy. You have the power and strength of the Holy Spirit. Most importantly, what you seek, love, and acceptance, you already have from Jesus. Take back your power and stand up against the lies and defeat the enemy!

How can you use your fighting spirit for good?

TAKE AWAY

You are God's strong mighty warrior! With God, you've already defeated the enemy!

ACTION

How can you use your fighting spirit for good?

YOU ARE GOD'S STRONG MIGHTY WARRIOR!

Day 7
MONTH 1

Day 7

Day 7

MONTH 2

Day 7

Day 7

MONTH 3

Day 7

Day 8

You are Victorious!

"And I sent terror ahead of you to drive out the two kings of the Amorites. It was not your swords or bows that brought you victory. I gave you land you had not worked on, and I gave you towns you did not build—the towns where you are now living. I gave you vineyards and olive groves for food, though you did not plant them."

Joshua 24:12-13 NLT

FROM YOUR FATHER

Although you are my warrior, I am your daddy, your protector. As you follow my lead, you will have victory over the enemy and in life. Seek my direction so that I can bless you and you won't have to struggle so much. I'll bless you with things you don't have to work hard for.

Day 8

THINK ABOUT

In and with Jesus you have victory. If you follow God's word, he will bless, protect, and give you victory in the situations you face; in school, with friends, on your job, or with family. Stop allowing the enemy to ruin and run your life. Take a hold of the VICTORY that's right in front of you!

What can you do to walk in victory over the enemy? In what way do you need to be obedient to God?

TAKE AWAY

YOU ARE VICTORIOUS!

Day 8

MONTH 1

Day 8

Day 8

MONTH 2

Day 8

Day 8

MONTH 3

Day 8

Day 9

You are a Lady or Gentleman!

"If you've gotten anything at all out of following Christ, if his love has made any difference in your life, if being in a community of the Spirit means anything to you, if you have a heart, if you care —then do me a favor: Agree with each other, love each other, be deep-spirited friends. Don't push your way to the front; don't sweet-talk your way to the top. Put yourself aside, and help others get ahead. Don't be obsessed with getting your own advantage. Forget yourselves long enough to lend a helping hand."
Philippians 2:1-4 MSG

FROM YOUR FATHER

You are the son or daughter of the King! You have a code of conduct you must follow. I created you like me: full of love, kindness and helpfulness. Just like I thought about you, and how much I love you, I sacrificed my only son for you. You are to love like me, serve like me and be humble, not thinking you are all that. You are a lady or gentleman; classy, not trashy.

Day 9

THINK ABOUT

A real lady and gentleman have a moral code higher than the common person. They don't brag about themselves and always does what's 'best' for others. They think about how they can help them. God's lady/gentleman, and you are, don't have to push their way to the top or do things for others to like them. They know their time will come and truly want to see others succeed. God's lady/gentleman isn't arrogant, proud or rude.

How can you be more like a lady or gentleman in your actions and attitude? Why is being a lady or gentleman important to God?

TAKE AWAY

You care about others and desire to help them; even before yourself.

YOU ARE A LADY OR GENTLEMAN!

Day 9

MONTH 1

Day 9

Day 9
MONTH 2

Day 9

Day 9

MONTH 3

Day 9

Day 10

You are a Blessing to Others!

In the same way, let your light shine before people in such a way that they will see your good actions and glorify your Father in heaven.

Matthew 5:16

FROM YOUR FATHER

You are beautiful from the inside out, my love. Let people see your inner beauty through your character and desire to bless others with your heart full of my love. Love on everyone, even your enemies. A life full of loving words and actions towards others is a life full of Me! You have it in you because you have my genes in you. My blood runs through your veins.

Day 10

THINK ABOUT

Shine bright like a diamond. You are precious, brilliant, and God's special treasure. Let his love shine in your good works so that others will want what you have: God. You were created to be a blessing to others: in your actions, how you talk to and treat others, towards your parents and friends. Shining bright for Jesus is living as he did; loving, helping, and being kind to others. He even prayed for his enemies.

How can you be a blessing to those around you?

_____
_____
_____
_____
_____
_____
_____
_____
_____
_____
_____

TAKE AWAY:

YOU ARE A BLESSING TO OTHERS.

Day 10
MONTH 1

Day 10

Day 10
MONTH 2

Day 10

Day 10
MONTH 3

Day 10

Day 11

You are Royalty!

And you have made them a kingdom and priests to our God, and they shall reign on the earth."

Revelations 5:10

FROM YOUR FATHER:

I love you so much that I sent my son for you; that you would be a part of my kingdom, my family, to reign as Kings and Queens on earth. You are leaders that represent my kingdom on earth. You are to bring my kingdom to this earth.

Day 11

THINK ABOUT

God gave you the power and authority as a king over your life and future. With that freedom and authority, use it for good. Reflect God's kingdom values in your everyday life by obeying Him and loving others. When you do, your influence, power, and blessings will increase.

How does knowing who you are and the position God's given you change how you think about yourself and how your actions affect others?

TAKE AWAY

You matter.

YOU ARE ROYALTY!

Day 11
MONTH 1

Day 11

Day 11

MONTH 2

Day 11

Day 11
MONTH 3

Day 11

Day 12

You are Loved!

"The LORD appeared to me (Israel) from ages past, saying, "I have loved you with an everlasting love; Therefore with lovingkindness I have drawn you and continued My faithfulness to you."

JEREMIAH 31:3 AMP

FROM YOUR FATHER

I'll love you forever; no matter what you do. When you disobey me, I will have mercy on you, but also give you tough love of consequences. When you choose to disobey me, my arms are still open to you waiting for you to come home. I will never leave or give up on you!

Day 12

THINK ABOUT

God loved you before you were born and still does. His love never fails. With his mercy, loving you even when you don't deserve, he's calling you back to him when you choose to go your own way. It's time for this long-distance relationship to end. You need to begin pursing your first love again with fire and passion. Call him every day. Spend time with him regularly. He is a jealous God. God's waiting for you to come back to his love.

Perfect love casts out fear. In what area have you walked away from God's love and not fully trusted him? Where have you taken over too much control? Journal your thoughts about God that has pushed you away.

TAKE AWAY

Even in your sin, even when you feel like you don't love God,

YOU ARE LOVED!

Day 12

MONTH 1

Day 12

Day 12
MONTH 2

Day 12

Day 12
MONTH 3

Day 12

Day 13

You are Valuable!

"Look at the birds. They don't plant or harvest or store food in barns, for your heavenly Father feeds them. And aren't you far more valuable to him than they are?
And if God cares so wonderfully for wildflowers that are here today and thrown into the fire tomorrow, he will certainly care for you. Why do you have so little faith?"

Matthew 6:26, 30 NLT

FROM YOUR FATHER

I am the Creator of heaven and earth. I care for, provide for, and have a purpose for all of my creation. I know your wants and your needs. I even know your thoughts; that's how close I am to you and how much you matter to me. Even the small things like birds and flowers I care for, but you, my darling, are far more important and valuable to me. If I take care of things as small as these, KNOW that I love you so much more, that I will take care of you even more! I'm your protector, provider, and promoter. You are my child and are so important to me.

Day 13

THINK ABOUT

Think of something special to you; something you treasure. How do you take care of it? You probably keep it in a special place so it doesn't get broken or dirty. If it does, you are quick to clean it or get it fixed. You don't want anyone to touch it because it's yours; you kind of have a jealous love for it because it's so important to you. This is how God; your loving Father sees you. He handpicked you, created you, and has a love that will never fade.

Write down how God treasures and takes care of you like you are a treasure. How does that make you feel?

TAKE AWAY

Don't ever forget how precious and worthy you are.

YOU ARE VALUABLE.

Day 13
MONTH 1

Day 13

Day 13
MONTH 2

Day 13

Day 13

MONTH 3

Day 13

Day 14

You are Uniquely and Wonderfully Made!

> "You made all the delicate, inner parts of my body and knit me together in my mother's womb. Thank you for making me so wonderfully complex! Your workmanship is marvelous—how well I know it."
>
> Psalms 139:13-14 NLT

FROM YOUR FATHER

I made you inside and out. Like a painter, I had a vision, carefully planned everything about you, and took my time creating you. Know how special and rare you are. You are my treasure. What I made is perfect! You are perfect in my eyes.

Day 14

THINK ABOUT

Millions of sperm and eggs float in a man and woman's body. Life is no mistake. Your father planned for you; when, to whom, and everything about you! He is the one who chose the exact egg and sperm to join and give you the specific character traits, personality, and passions you have. He's over the top extravagant with everything he does. Know that you were chosen and carefully thought of; God doesn't make mistakes.

What don't you like about yourself? Write it down and envision how God sees that quality as something positive.

TAKE AWAY

YOU ARE UNIQUELY AND WONDERFULLY MADE! Don't ever question it. Don't focus on what you think are flaws. Focus on the beauty your Father created in you!

Day 14

MONTH 1

Day 14

Day 14

MONTH 2

Day 14

Day 14

MONTH 3

Day 14

Day 15

You are Gifted!

Each of you should use whatever gift you have received to serve others, as faithful stewards of God's grace in its various forms.

1 Peter 4:10

FROM YOUR FATHER:

Love, I've created you with a unique gift and purpose. Use the thing that comes natural to you to help other people, not just yourself. Everyone has different talents. Use yours wisely or I'll get someone else that's willing.

Day 15

THINK ABOUT

Did you know that everyone was created with certain talents? You shouldn't be jealous of anyone's gift, or try to be like them. God created you specifically how He wanted, to accomplish a specific purpose and help many people. You're not talented because of anything you've done, but because your daddy loved you so much, he wanted to give you something special to represent him on earth. Be faithful and use your gift for others or you will lose the opportunity.

What comes easy to you? What are you good at? Pray and ask God to show you. If you know your gift, write down how you can use your gift to help others.

TAKE AWAY

Use your gifts to make your daddy proud!

YOU'RE GIFTED!

Day 15

MONTH 1

Day 15

Day 15

MONTH 2

Day 15

Day 15

MONTH 3

Day 15

Day 16

You are Destined for Greatness!

"You are the light of [Christ to] the world. A city set on a hill cannot be hidden; nor does anyone light a lamp and put it under a basket, but on a lampstand, and it gives light to all who are in the house. Let your light shine before men in such a way that they may see your good deeds and moral excellence, and [recognize and honor and] glorify your Father who is in heaven."

MATTHEW 5:14-16 AMP

FROM YOUR FATHER:

Because you are my child; you have a platform of influence. People are watching you. Because your father is the king and your brother is the infamous Jesus, you are expected to do great things. You have a reputation to live up to.

Day 16

THINK ABOUT

Although it may not seem fair, people of high stature or celebrity, are expected to live at a higher standard. You know that Beyoncé's daughter is destined for greatness just because of who her mother is. Everyone's watching Sasha and Malia Obama to see what they'll do. Expectations are high. People want to be like them and wish the Obamas were their parents. You are in the same category with Blue Ivy, Sasha, and Malia. Your daddy is the ultimate King.

What does it look like to live at a high standard? How does God expect you to talk, respond, and behave? Be specific.

TAKE AWAY

Shine your light to reflect your daddy's influence and power.

YOU'RE DESTINED FOR GREATNESS!

Day 16

MONTH 1

Day 16

Day 16

MONTH 2

Day 16

Day 16

MONTH 3

Day 16

Day 17

You are Powerful!

"I can do all things [which He has called me to do] through Him who strengthens and empowers me [to fulfill His purpose—I am self-sufficient in Christ's sufficiency; I am ready for anything and equal to anything through Him who infuses me with inner strength and confident peace.]"

PHILIPPIANS 4:13 AMP

FROM YOUR FATHER

I am the one who gives you the power to handle life's situations and accomplish your dreams. What I call you to do, I will help you through it. I have equipped you with everything you need to be successful in life. You have the same power that raised Jesus from the dead living in you (the Holy Spirit). You can handle anything life throws your way because I'm with you and in you.

Day 17

THINK ABOUT

Have you ever felt down in the dumps? Have you ever listened to music that helped you feel better, or had a conversation with someone that encouraged you? Your father knows what you need and is always with you in your struggle. He can put a song in your spirit, send someone to give you a word of encouragement, or have the Holy Spirit give you direction and courage to do what you need to do in order to have victory over your situations. Imagine how much power it took to raise Jesus from the dead. That sounds like magic. You have the same power within you! Use it. #RessurectionPower

Jesus defeated Satan with the Word of God. Find a scripture that speaks God's promise about your situation, write it down, and speak it boldly each day.

TAKE AWAY

Don't let your circumstances, sin, or your friends control you.

YOU ARE POWERFUL.

Day 17
MONTH 1

Day 17

Day 17

MONTH 2

Day 17

Day 17
MONTH 3

Day 17

Day 18

You are a King or Queen!

> *"...and from Jesus Christ. He is the faithful witness to these things, the first to rise from the dead, and the ruler of all the kings of the world. All glory to him who loves us and has freed us from our sins by shedding his blood for us. He has made us a Kingdom of priests for God his Father. All glory and power to him forever and ever! Amen."*
>
> Revelation 1:5-6 NLT

FROM YOUR FATHER

I love you so much that I have entrusted to you to be kings (rulers) of this world. As my king, you are a representation of me and my power in the earth. My love has cleansed and freed you from your sins through the blood of Jesus, so that you may operate in my power and authority. You are free to rule for me.

THINK ABOUT

How does one become a king? Unlike the president being voted in, a King's position is inherited. You have to be of the same bloodline as the king; even closer, his child. Because of

Day 18

God's love for you, he has brought you into his family bloodline through the sacrifice of Jesus. You are now a co-heir with Christ to receive kingship to rule on earth.

How does knowing who your father is and the fact that He has chosen you to inherit His power and authority as king change the way you think about yourself? How will this new mindset affect how you live?

TAKE AWAY

By the love of your father through the blood of Jesus,

YOU ARE A KING OR QUEEN!

MONTH 1

Day 18

Day 18

MONTH 2

Day 18

Day 18

MONTH 3

Day 18

Day 18

Day 19

You are God's Strong Mighty Warrior!

For You have girded me with strength for battle; You have subdued under me those who rose up against me.

Psalms 18:39

FROM YOUR FATHER

I am your strength. My power is made perfect when you realize you need me and that you are weak by yourself. Come to me so that I can recharge you for warfare. Every day is a battle of good and evil. You have choices to make. Remember whose army you fight for. You can do all things as you lean on me for your strength. Know that you are on the winning team.

Day 19

THINK ABOUT

To gird means to secure (a garment or sword) on the body with a belt or band. Another definition says to encircle (a person or part of the body) with a belt or band. God has encircled you with His strength. He has made it so secure that the enemy can't hurt you when he strikes a blow. You are stronger than you think; stronger than the enemy thinks. The verse repeats that God has... not you! God is the one that gives you strength, makes it secure, and gives you victory over the enemy. Humble yourself and submit to his authority so that you can walk in victory.

God says that you must humble yourself before He will exalt (honor) you. Why is it important to know that it's God's strength and not your own that wins your battles?

TAKE AWAY

YOU ARE GOD'S STRONG MIGHTY WARRIOR;
not your own. He gives you strength/power to have victory over life's situations.

Day 19

MONTH 1

Day 19

Day 19

MONTH 2

Day 19

Day 19

MONTH 3

Day 19

Day 20

You are Victorious!

"For every child of God defeats this evil world, and we achieve this victory through our faith. And who can win this battle against the world? Only those who believe that Jesus is the Son of God."

1 John 5:4-5 NLT

FROM YOUR FATHER

You are my child. You show your love for me by obeying me. When you do, you can have victory over any situation that comes your way. You defeat evil by believing in Jesus and trusting me. I want you to win every battle, but it's up to you. Know that I am with you in your battles and I am bigger than your problems and enemies.

Day 20

THINK ABOUT

A lot of people believe in Jesus and believe they are a child of God, but God's word says that you are a child of God if you love him. True children of God obey him. Obedience stands in the way between you being victorious.

What is one way that you can operate in obedience so that you can have victory in your situation?

TAKE AWAY

IN CHRIST, YOU ARE VICTORIOUS.

Day 20

MONTH 1

Day 20

Day 20

MONTH 2

Day 20

Day 20
MONTH 3

Day 20

Day 21

You are a Lady or Gentleman!

Let us behave properly as in the day, not in carousing (unbecoming behavior because of drinking) and drunkenness, not in sexual promiscuity and sensuality (physical/sexual pleasure), not in strife (fighting) and jealousy.

Romans 13:13

FROM YOUR FATHER

You are my child. People are watching you. You represent ME: walk as I walk; talk like I talk. Your body is MY temple. Don't give it away. Keep yourself pure for the one I have for you: your spouse. We don't excessively drink alcohol. We're not loud or rude, and we don't fight. There's no reason for you to be jealous of anyone because you have access to every blessing and special treatment because you are MY child.

Day 21

THINK ABOUT

In today's society, there's such a fine line between right and wrong, moral and immoral. Don't follow what's going on in society. You should be set apart: look different, respond differently, act differently. A lady/gentleman treats people with respect, speaks with tact, is kind, and peaceful. He/she doesn't get drunk, use their bodies inappropriately, give themselves away to others, or engage in fighting.

What area do you need to more of a lady or gentleman? Choose one thing you will do this week to step into your new identity. Journal your progress this week.

TAKE AWAY

YOU ARE A LADY/GENTLEMAN;
act like it. You are a walking billboard for your father, the king!

Day 21
MONTH 1

Day 21

Day 21

MONTH 2

Day 21

Day 21
MONTH 3

Day 21

Day 22

You are a Blessing to Others!

> "I will make you into a great nation. I will bless you and make you famous, and you will be a blessing to others."
>
> Genesis 12:2 NLT

FROM YOUR FATHER

As your daddy I want you to be great! I want your life to positively impact others. I have so much in store for you. I want to bless you so much. Sometimes it may seem like others are getting blessed, but when you're ready and able to handle it, your blessings are on the way! I expect that when I bless you, you bless others.

Day 22

THINK ABOUT

It is God who makes you successful: not you. He gives you the gifts and ability to gain wealth and stature. The gift he put in you will bring you in front of great opportunities and positions. The reason for this is for you to be a blessing to others, not just yourself. People are waiting for you!

What is your why? You know what you want, but why do you want it? If your why is just about you, ask God to change your heart. He wants you to be a river, not a reservoir.

TAKE AWAY

As God blesses you,

YOU ARE A BLESSING TO OTHERS.

Day 22

MONTH 1

Day 22

Day 22
MONTH 2

Day 22

Day 22

MONTH 3

Day 22

Day 23

You are Royalty!

> "So you have not received a spirit that makes you fearful slaves. Instead, you received God's Spirit when he adopted you as his own children. Now we call him, "Abba, Father." For his Spirit joins with our spirit to affirm that we are God's children. And since we are his children, we are his heirs. In fact, together with Christ we are heirs of God's glory. But if we are to share his glory, we must also share his suffering."
>
> Romans 8:15-17 NLT

FROM YOUR FATHER

You are my child. I didn't give you a spirit of fear. You don't need to fear because you have my power and authority running through your veins. Your last name is Royalty! Stand firm in who you are and know that judgmental haters will try to oppose you. Life won't always be peachy but know that I'll be with you and my name is GREATER!

Day 23

THINK ABOUT

Slaves live in fear of their masters. Slaves have no power or authority. Slaves don't have any access to freedom. However, you are the opposite of a slave. You are a son/daughter! You live in the palace. You eat at the king's table! You have access to everything that is the king's: blessings, honor, favor, and persecution. Kings have enemies too. Everyday people judge him and act unfavorably to him. Because you bear His name, you too will face unfair treatment and judgment. Be prepared to respond like a true royal person: with love, kindness, respect, and tact. Know that the only opinion that matters is God's.

How will you respond to persecution? How does your response need to change as you begin to recognize that you are royalty?

TAKE AWAY

Know who you are and stand firm in your position.

YOU ARE ROYALTY.

Day 23

MONTH 1

Day 23

Day 23

MONTH 2

Day 23

Day 23

MONTH 3

Day 23

Day 24

You are Loved!

This is how we know what love is: Jesus Christ laid down his life for us. And we ought to lay down our lives for our brothers. If anyone has material possessions and sees his brother in need but has no pity on him, how can the love of God be in him? Dear children, let us not love with words or tongue but with actions and in truth."

1 John 3:16-18

FROM YOUR FATHER

I love you so much that I offered your brother, at the time, my only son just for you. Family is so important to me. The fact that I'd give up my family just for you to be a part of my family is tremendous! I never wanted to see my son die, but I imagined the promise that I'd have you as my child too, that I spent a night of weeping so I could spend eternity loving you. That is how much you mean to me. As I've lavished my love for you, I expect you to love others in the same manner. You represent me to the world. When people see your life, they should see ME.

Day 24

THINK ABOUT

Not only does the Father love you with an unconditional, sacrificial, death kind of love, Jesus loves you that much too! Not only one, but 2 people love you beyond death. That's amazing. This kind of love should keep you from falling for fake love from other people. This is real love. You are worthy of the same kind of love and appreciation from someone that wants a relationship with you. Don't allow people to minimize your worth. If the King of Kings, the creator of the world will die for you, don't let anyone treat you less than. You also must treat others with the same love and value. They are of the same worth to God as you are.

"People know who your daddy is by how you love others. Even love the people you don't like with the same unconditional love God gives you. Although He knew you'd go against Him, He still gave His life for you. Who do you need to do the same for? What will you commit to doing to show the love of God to someone who is unlovable?"

TAKE AWAY

You are expected to give that same love to those you love and those you don't!

YOU ARE LOVED.

Day 24
MONTH 1

Day 24

Day 24

MONTH 2

Day 24

Day 24
MONTH 3

Day 24

Day 25

You are Valuable!

Proverbs 31:10-13 A wife of noble character who can find? She is worth far more than rubies. Her husband has full confidence in her and lacks nothing of value. She brings him good, not harm, all the days of her life.

FROM YOUR FATHER:

You are husband/wife material. Your value is that of a rare treasure. Not many people are like you. Regardless of what society says is important or acceptable, you know better. You're not like the world; you are the heir to the throne. Your net worth far exceeds celebrities and millionaires. You're worth far more than just money. Your character stands out above the rest: your hard work ethic, love, serving, and giving spirit, tenacity, faithfulness amongst other qualities make you unique. I've instilled these traits in you. You may not be exhibiting them now, but the time has come to show the world who you truly are.

Day 25

THINK ABOUT

Other words for valuable are precious items, costly articles, prized possessions, treasures.

- Think of something that you'd keep in a safe; things that you would guard with your life. God values you so much more than that! You are precious to him. He'd protect you with his life. Oh yeah, he died for you. That's how much he values you.
- People pay a lot of money for diamonds, cars, and houses. You are worth more than these costly articles.
- You are "all-powerful God," "creator of the universe," "can do what I want" and "speak things into existence" God's prized possession... He could have anything he wants, but he chose YOU. He spoke you into existence. He formed you just how he wanted. He'd do anything for you.
- People search to the end of the earth to find treasure. Treasure they hope to be there. Even though they're unsure, they believe the treasure is valuable enough that if they find it, their life would be changed. People will protect and kill for rare treasure. Guess what? Even when you leave God, He comes after you. You are his treasure. He will stop at nothing to find you and bring you home. He will guard you with his life and wouldn't sell you for anything!

Now that you know your value, how will you shine bright like a diamond? What will you stop allowing people to do to you because you know your true worth?

TAKE AWAY

YOU ARE VALUABLE to god and there's nothing you can do about it.

Day 25

MONTH 1

Day 25

Day 25

MONTH 2

Day 25

Day 25

MONTH 3

Day 25

Day 26

You are Uniquely and Wonderfully Made!

"For we are God's masterpiece. He has created us anew in Christ Jesus, so we can do the good things he planned for us long ago."
Ephesians 2:10 NLT

Song of Songs 4:7 *"You are altogether beautiful, my darling; there is no flaw in you."*

FROM YOUR FATHER:

Although your mother birthed you, I am the one who dreamed about you and designed every part of who you are. Picasso has nothing on me. You are flawless in my eyes. You're beautiful from the inside - out. No matter what you've done in the past, the reputation you've built, the mistakes you've made, I am using those imperfections to shape and mold you into a new masterpiece. It is the power of the Holy Spirit that transforms the old you, into the Real you. Now go and do what I've called you to do: live a life of significance using the gift I've created you with. Expand My kingdom on earth!

Day 26

THINK ABOUT

Anyone can paint a picture, but not everyone can create a masterpiece. A masterpiece only has that title because a lot of people agree on how sought after, intriguing, and breathtaking a piece of art is. You are a piece of art that everyone admires, wants, and reveres. The master artist created you anew once you believed in Jesus. His purpose was so that you would represent his kingdom agenda in the earth through the unique gift and passion he's placed in you. Like a masterpiece, you are one of a kind! If you don't know your purpose, ask your creator. Until it is made known to you, glorify God in your current position by loving Him above all and loving others.

What steps do you need to take to begin walking like the masterpiece you were created to be?

TAKE AWAY

YOU ARE UNIQUELY AND WONDERFULLY MADE
for a purpose.

Day 26

MONTH 1

Day 26

Day 26

MONTH 2

Day 26

Day 26

MONTH 3

Day 26

Day 27

You are Gifted and Destined for Greatness!

A man's gift [given in love or courtesy] makes room for him and brings him before great men."

PROVERBS 18:16 AMP

FROM YOUR FATHER

You have my genes in you. My gifts are your gifts. Like father like child. There is at least one gift (natural ability) that I've given you for you to use to serve others in order to build My kingdom on earth. Give it away because others need it; they're waiting for it. Don't hoard it to yourself. When you use your gift unselfishly for others, I will open up doors for your gift to be magnified in the presence of powerful people.

Day 27

THINK ABOUT

Jesus didn't set out to become famous. He came to only do the Father's will. His heart was for people and he performed miracles to help people. His motive was of love, not greed or self. He had a gift of compassion and healing power. That gift brought him in front of masses of people. He's known for many miracles. He used his gift, not sat on it. Almost every time Jesus is spoken of in the Bible, he was teaching or healing. You have to use the gift God's given you with a selfless heart and God will exalt you and your influence will increase.

You'll only walk in your destiny of greatness if you are humble, have pure motives and use your gift for the benefit of others. Humility is a strength, not a weakness. It is a quiet confidence in the God in you to work for you and make you great. It is trusting in God's protection, provision. And promises. Write down what it means for you to be humble and what you need to do to become a person of humility.

TAKE AWAY

YOU ARE GIFTED AND DESTINED FOR GREATNESS.

Day 27

MONTH 1

Day 27

Day 27
MONTH 2

Day 27

Day 27
MONTH 3

Day 27

Day 28

You are a Powerful King or Queen!

"The Son radiates God's own glory and expresses the very character of God, and he sustains everything by the mighty power of his command. "Hebrews 1:3

"For you were buried with Christ when you were baptized. And with him you were raised to new life because you trusted the mighty power of God, who raised Christ from the dead." Colossians 2:12

"For God has not given us a spirit of fear and timidity, but of power, love and self – discipline." 2 Timothy 1:7

"For the Kingdom of God is not just a lot of talk; it is living by God's power." 1 Corinthians 4:20

FROM YOUR FATHER

You are my child. You have my blood and DNA flowing through your body. I've given you supernatural power to glorify me. You have spoken word authority. The same resurrection power of my spirit lives in you. It's up to you to operate in it. I've led you to the river; it's time for you to jump in and swim. Don't be scared. Apply what I've taught you and bring the light to this dark world. It won't be easy, but it's

Day 28

necessary. The world is searching, longing, and waiting for the real King to take his rightful position and lead with power and effectiveness.

THINK ABOUT

A kingdom can't operate without a strong King that knows their purpose and power. An heir can't take their rightful position until they've proven that they're mature and ready to lead. You've been created and chosen for such a time as this. Think about your favorite superhero. What was he or she like? Why are they your favorite? You have superpowers given to you by the ultimate superhero! You are even more powerful than King T'challa from Black Panther. It is your responsibility to use your power for God and responsibly.

What character trait do you have that needs to be pruned because it doesn't represent the character of God? What one thing will you commit to walk in your new identity?

TAKE AWAY

YOU ARE A POWERFUL KING OR QUEEN.

Day 28
MONTH 1

Day 28

Day 28
MONTH 2

Day 28

Day 28
MONTH 3

Day 28

Day 29

You are God's Strong Mighty Warrior! You are Victorious!

"When the men of Judah attacked, the Lord gave them victory over the Canaanites and Perizzites, and they killed 10,000 enemy warriors at the town of Bezek."
Judges 1:4 NLT

"You are the one who gives us victory over our enemies; you disgrace those who hate us."
Psalms 44:7 NLT

You will pursue your enemies, and they will fall by the sword before you.
Leviticus 26:7

FROM YOUR FATHER

Since the beginning, there's been a war between Satan and heaven. His goal is to take you out because you have what he wants: My name, My power, and My authority. You've been armed for this war and with Heaven's armies behind you, you have victory over the enemy. His one goal is to stop you from knowing who you are, your power and your purpose. It's attack mode time. Be prepared for the

Day 29

enemy to attack and don't react, but respond according to my Word. You can do this. I got you. You've already won.

THINK ABOUT:

A warrior is always prepared for when the enemy will strike. He is watching and waiting. You know your weaknesses and struggles. Put the word of God in you (reading it daily) concerning your weak areas so that you are ready to attack with the Word when Satan tries to hit you with lies. Pray Ephesians 6:11 daily and be on guard. Your weapons aren't physical, but spiritual. They are able to pull down strongholds and every darkness that comes against the Word of God. The battle is not with people but in your mind. If he gets your mind, he has you. If he gets you to doubt and question God, he'll keep you from walking in your power and destiny!

TAKE AWAY

Before you see the victory, know that you've already won! Now step into your destiny!

YOU ARE GOD'S STRONG MIGHTY WARRIOR. You are victorious!

Day 29

MONTH 1

Day 29

Day 29

MONTH 2

Day 29

Day 29

MONTH 3

Day 29

Day 30

You are a Lady or Gentleman, a Blessing to Others! You are Royalty!

> "But the Holy Spirit produces this kind of fruit in our lives: love, joy, peace, patience, kindness, goodness, faithfulness, gentleness, and self-control. There is no law against these things!
> Since we are living by the Spirit, let us follow the Spirit's leading in every part of our lives. Let us not become conceited, or provoke one another, or be jealous of one another."
> Galatians 5:22-23, 25-26 NLT

FROM YOUR FATHER:

Just because you grow in age doesn't make you a lady or gentleman. Living by the power of the Holy Spirit produces the character I put in you. No matter what situation comes your way, I want you to handle it with maturity and grace. Don't allow anyone or anything to get you out of character; that's Satan's goal, so he can come to me and make accusations against you. There's no need to think more highly of yourself than you should. There's always going to be someone that's better than you and you're not in competition with them anyway. Operate in love, kindness, peacefulness,

Day 30

patience, faithfulness, and self-control and you'll shine bright like a diamond...

THINK ABOUT

Jealous people envy what others have because they feel less than. You are loved, valuable, and uniquely made. You are gifted, destined for greatness, and powerful. You're a strong mighty warrior that is victorious. On top of that, you are more than a woman or man, you're a lady/gentleman. What an honor to be of the royal family. Act like it. Talk like it. Walk with confidence because you know who you are and who your daddy is. Become what you're called to be: Royalty!

How do you feel differently about who you are based on what your Father says you are? Share your new identity!

TAKE AWAY:

YOU ARE A LADY/GENTLEMAN.

YOU ARE A BLESSING TO OTHERS.

YOU ARE ROYALTY!

Day 30

MONTH 1

Day 30

Day 30

MONTH 2

Day 30

Day 30

MONTH 3

Day 30

Daily I Am Affirmation

(Look in the mirror and speak this aloud daily. "As a man thinks in his heart, so is he." "Speak the things that are not (yet) as though they already are.")

- ❖ I AM Loved
- ❖ I AM Valuable
- ❖ I AM Uniquely and Wonderfully Made
- ❖ I AM Gifted
- ❖ I AM Destined for Greatness
- ❖ I AM Powerful
- ❖ I AM a King or Queen
- ❖ I AM God's Strong Mighty Warrior
- ❖ I AM Victorious
- ❖ I AM a Lady or Gentleman
- ❖ I AM a Blessing to Others
- ❖ I AM Royalty

www.ingramcontent.com/pod-product-compliance
Lightning Source LLC
Chambersburg PA
CBHW060822050426
42453CB00008B/543